"MY SISTER AND I"

"My sister and I remember still…
The home that was all our own until…
But we don't talk about that.

We're learning to forget the fear…
We're almost happy over here
But sometimes we wake…and cry
(But we don't talk about that.)

My sister and I recall the day
We said goodbye then sailed away
And we think of (those who) had to stay
But we don't talk about that."*

*Abridged lyrics from *My Sister and I* (1941)
By Hy Zaret, Joan Whitney, Alex Kramer

SIX YEARS
FOREVER LOST

THE TESTIMONY OF
MANYA FRYDMAN PEREL

AS TOLD TO MARC JOEL ADELMAN

Date of Publication: 2011-05-01

<u>DEDICATION</u>

To my dearest and special grandchildren; Evan, Yael, Andrew, Daniel, Rina and Jeffrey. For their future and the future generations to come. With all my love.

Bubbe

TABLE OF CONTENTS

ACKNOWLEDGMENTS

This testimony was not only a collaboration of spirit and intent but a direct result of the determination and courage of Manya Frydman Perel. As you read her story, you will recognize that the meaning of the above terms, spirit, determination, and courage, are written into the literal text as well as between the lines of the narrative. I took my cue from Manya's twelve page testimony; from her interview included in Steven Spielberg's Shoah Foundation archives at the University of Southern California; and the many hours and days I spent in Manya's home probing and gleaning the intimate information necessary for a most truthful account. My intent was to write in such a way as to capture her Eastern European voice so that when you read the text you will also hear her voice. The fact that she plied me with snacks of her delicious *Komish* bread should not sway you from the opinion that I was forthright and honest giving an account of her life that was the Holocaust.

I would like to thank Esther Surden, a tireless supporter of Holocaust survivors who did the initial editing and my life long best of friends Dr. Sidney and Lois Clearfield who read through the manuscript and gave me sound advice. Sid is a past International Director of B'nai Brith Youth and past International Executive Vice-President of B'nai Brith. My appreciation to Jim Dougherty an artisan of the print industry for his creative cover designs and invaluable help. Thanks to Steven Adelman for helping with the technical task of formatting the book. Thanks also to Manuel Wamsler, a young volunteer for the Action Reconciliation for Service and Peace (ARSP) for assisting me in research. Special thanks to Sylvia and Mark Wagman and Marvin and Lois Perel, Manya's children, for their support and approval.

I verified as much of Manya's story as feasible but ultimately this is her saga subject to her interpretation of the facts as she remembers them. Most of my facts came from my research and, particularly, <u>The Book of Radom</u>, Alfred Lipton, ed. Liberty Press, New York 1963. The book is full of primary resources confirming Manya's experience. My inspiration was also derived from the lives of all Holocaust survivors that I have come to know and work with as an educator and volunteer for the Holocaust Awareness Museum and Education Center. Manya's testimony is not just in the telling, it is in the way she lives her life with enthusiasm, intellect and dignity.

Marc Joel Adelman

AUTHOR'S PREFACE

I met Manya Frydman Perel without knowing one thing about her other than she was a Holocaust survivor. I was a new volunteer for the Holocaust Awareness Museum and Education Center in Philadelphia, Pennsylvania. I escorted her to a play one night. It was a play about women Holocaust survivors of concentration camps. Since Manya had survived eight camps, she was introduced to the theater audience and then, after the performance, she remained for a Q & A session.

Manya Frydman Perel, octogenarian and slight of stature, gave the theater group her testimony in a strong accented voice that projected as well if not better than most of the actors on stage. Since that night, I have facilitated Manya as well as a dozen other survivors in presenting their first hand testimony to the most horrific crimes perpetrated on mankind by other human beings, the Holocaust.

I am in awe of her ability to speak to thousands and tell her story over and over again. Manya was forced to be courageous seventy years ago when she lived minute by minute, hour by hour, and day by day not knowing whether she would live or die. Today, she chooses to be courageous by reliving her loss of culture, family and dignity every time she presents her story publicly. Every day, Manya continues to seek opportunities to become an extraordinary spokesperson as a witness to the injustices of the past with the hope that mankind will recognize their mistakes so that there will be a future free of genocide and state sponsored evil.

As I immersed myself in Manya's account of her Holocaust history, as well as the testimony of other survivors, I had no intention writing about any particular Holocaust scenario. But Manya's saga stands out, above all, as a tale of determination, courage, and resistance. She has faced both the evil and the good in human kind. Manya wanted her story written for her family and friends. I wanted her testimony recognized and received by a larger audience. I wanted to write about her Holocaust experience for the example it sets for all of us today and for future generations.

While living a stressful and fearful life in a ghetto; lying cramped in death camp barracks; standing in ankle deep mud for hours; shivering in the worst winter conditions; suffocating under a pile of bodies fighting for a crumb of bread; and parading in a death march with women who fell dead every few steps, Manya promised her family members, who didn't survive the Holocaust, that she would continue to remember and honor them with her last breath. I am humbled to help her in the effort.

MJA

The following poem is not my creation but something I remember from reading at some point in my life, when I found it difficult to forget the words. It comes very close to expressing my experience, my life during the Holocaust. I honor the poet. I honor the creativity and the humanity in the expression of their experience; this person who could have very well been my friend in Radom, Poland. I appreciate my life and every minute I have now is just a miracle.

Manya Frydman Perel

By day I can escape
Never by night.
I return to where
The shadows are long
And the darkness surreal.
I return to where the
Earth is mingled with the
Ashes of innocent souls.
I lie still among the corpses
Eerie, solitary and cold.
I feel boots marching
I hear rifles shooting
I wake in terror and shake.
I return to where electric fences
Keep the world away. I lay
So lonely all night and day.
Shrill scenarios rend the air
Does not anyone care?
I wait in fear and shake
I return to where fumes leap to
Heaven
And smoke covers the sky.
I sit quietly on the ground
And watch so many die.
The stench of death
In every breath.
I wait and shake.

PROLOGUE

My name is Manya Frydman Perel. I was born Mania Frydman in Radom, Poland on August 28th, 1924. I am here alive by a miracle to tell my story and give testimony to surviving the greatest human catastrophe on earth, the Holocaust. Hitler and his Nazis committed the most brutal crimes against humanity. They succeeded in the near destruction of European Jewry by a systematic and premeditated slaughter. I am a survivor of eight concentration camps. I, myself, call them death camps. For six years, during WWII, when Hitler and the Nazis came to power, I had no life. At first in the Radom ghettos and later in eight inhumane Nazi concentration camps, I suffered humiliation, torture, and hunger. Why? Because I was born a Jew.

I lost my parents and most of my family but it was my destiny to survive this great catastrophe and give witness to the murderous immoral behavior of the Nazi regime. Despite the horrible conditions, I was not selfish. I risked my life to save others. On May 1st, 1945, I was liberated by the Russian forces. This is my individual account, as I remember it; my personal hell on earth and what the <u>world</u> has come to know as, the Holocaust.

CHAPTER ONE

Normalcy: Family and Faith

It started in the year of 1939. At that time, I was a teenager like any others with dreams for the future. I lived with my family in the city of Radom, Poland. Radom was a city with 90,000 people a third of who were Jewish. It was a 1000 year old Jewish center of culture, commerce, and spirituality.[1] I was living with a nice family, my family. My parents, Abraham and Hanna, owned a bakery one of the largest of many Jewish owned bakeries in Radom. Everyone knew Frydman's bakery.[2]

My father and mother worked in the bakery and, along with my siblings, I helped. We were five boys and five girls, ten children in all; my brothers, Morris, Leon, Shevech, Herschel, and Itsik; and my sisters, Shifra, Regina, Pola, and Bronia. We were all together and happy to be together. We worked very hard in Radom. Life was not easy. I was the youngest and most pampered of all my siblings and so very much loved by everybody. It was a good comfortable feeling of love. Though life in Radom was hard, we managed to have a life of respect, comfort and

Parents Hanna and Abraham.
Died in the Treblinka extermination camp.

togetherness. We spoke two languages in our home, Polish and Yiddish. I lived with my orthodox parents and we observed the Sabbath and Jewish holidays. My mother was working in the home to nourish and comfort her children. We kept kosher. My father went to synagogue. I went to public school. I went to Hebrew school and learned to read from the prayer book. I was a good student hoping that someday I would be able to go to high school and later to college to have a good education.

There was always enough food on the table. I had bananas and oranges, which were always scarce, and took them to school with me to share with my friends. Then the shortage of bread began. My parents helped poor people, both Jews and Poles, by giving them some bread when they saw the need.

There were anti-Semitic violent mob attacks, pogroms, in Poland perpetrated by Poles before the Holocaust, most notably in Przytyk in 1936.[3] Relatives and friends came to our home from small towns or villages such as Przytyk; some driven out by pogroms others on personal matters, perhaps to see doctors. They slept and ate in our home and they were always welcomed.

My sister Regina personally took bread to relatives in small towns around Radom to help. My brothers risked their lives traveling to the city of Lublin where the mills of grain were stored. They brought home flour to make more bread for the hungry people; starving Polish people, Jewish and gentile, who were standing in line the whole night to get a loaf of bread. The Polish people, the Gentiles, the help in our bakery needed my father and he was charitable so they respected him.

When I grew up, I belonged to a Zionist organization: the Zabotynsky's.[4] My friends and my brothers and sisters were all in the same organization. We went to meetings to plan to go to Palestine. I believed that every people should have a country of their own and we should have Palestine. My father didn't go to meetings because he worked very hard to make a living and to help the poor people in Radom. Zabotynsky, the leader of the group, spoke in stirring words. He warned us to go out of Poland. We learned we had to have a country of our own in Palestine. We hoped that someday we would achieve our dream to enter our own land and build a country.

All of my brothers and sisters lived at home. Two of them, Morris and Regina, got married and

Brother Morris and sister-in-law Regina.
Escaped to Argentina.

moved out in 1937. We were together and there was enough bread on the table. It was a happy life; a normal life. We respected our parents, other people and in this way we grew up with respect.

I remember an incident in school. One friend's mother passed away. I couldn't imagine how she could live without a mother. When I came home, I looked for my mother. I hugged her. I was happy she was alive. I couldn't imagine losing my mother. Later on, I lost my mother. She was gassed and cremated in the death camp, Treblinka.

I was a teenager before the occupation. I had my friends. We had dreams of the future. We would grow up, meet a nice young man and get married. Those were our dreams. I didn't know about anti-Semitism when the Nazis came. When the Nazis marched into Radom, no one was a friend anymore.

CHAPTER TWO

The Occupation: Incomprehensible

I remember the years of 1939-1945. Those were years of humiliation, starvation, and torture. They were the years when death would have been a blessing for those who were still alive. We did not know that such things would or could happen to us. Our minds could not comprehend that in the 20th Century, in a world of civilization or culture including German composers such as Schumann; philosophers like Hesse; the physicist Einstein; and writers such as Heine; how such people as the Germans could perpetrate torture on so many human beings.

Many Jewish people came in from Germany and said they had to be evacuated. The Nazis told them they didn't ever want the Polish Jews to return to Germany.[5] It was then that we heard about Hitler and how he came to power. The Jewish population in Radom became very restless. We couldn't imagine, we couldn't comprehend how or what would happen.

CHAPTER THREE

Normalcy: Overrun

When the Nazis invaded Poland on September 1st, 1939, we heard the first signs of danger. There were a few bombs thrown from planes at the airport. There was chaos. We knew the Germans started the war and our lives would change. We heard rumors that the town of Kielce was captured forty miles away from Radom on September 5th. Many Jewish people started to leave Radom in fear of their lives.

On September 8th, the Germans marched in. From the very first day, panic started in Radom. I can still hear the sound of the soldier's boots as they came to beat us and chase us out of our homes. The Nazis shouted, "Out! *Raus* from the house!" They came to the houses and they took out the young men for labor. The soldiers sent them out for difficult work to dig ditches the Germans needed for war. The Germans killed people. Every day there was killing.

When the Nazis invaded, life started to be most difficult and impossible for the Radom Jews. It

Manya and hoola-hoop with sisters
Pola and Bronia

didn't take long for them to take action against the Jews. It was days, weeks, and then months. They confiscated our homes. We were forbidden to go to school. We were forbidden to walk on the side walks when the German soldiers passed. We were forbidden to go to the parks to play or sit. We couldn't listen to radio or go to the cinema. We were ordered to wear white armbands with the Star of David.[6]

Then, the rationing of bread began. The hunger started and lines formed to get bread. The Nazis gave us slight portions of flour to make bread. We had to stop baking because there was not enough flour to feed the people. Citizens of Radom were standing in line begging for bread.[7]

We had three stores. Stores were run by my father, my sister Shifra and one by my brother Herschel. We lived, in an apartment behind the main store at #17 on Jacka Malczewskiego Street. The entire family was under occupation except for one brother, Morris, who gained visas to go to Argentina with his wife, Regina, and child, Marek. We waited to go out also but we couldn't get away. It got very bad. It was impossible and we couldn't escape. The Nazis closed the borders and they made sure nobody could go out of Poland. We couldn't go to Palestine.

Brother Herschel in Polish uniform.
Died in Treblinka extermination camp.

CHAPTER FOUR

The Ghetto: No Way Out

Throughout 1940 and 1941, we lived and worked on a street outside the Jewish ghetto that had been made in Radom. In 1942, however, the Nazis determined that we leave the gentile street and enter the ghetto because our home and bakery was supposed to be inside.[8] A Polish man, who owned a bakery, came to my father and said we should switch bakeries because we had a bakery outside the ghetto and his store was in the ghetto. We would go in his bakery where the ghetto was formed and live behind the store also. I clung to my parents holding a few belongings and we left our home, the only home I knew.

The Nazis herded us into a small ghetto, the Szpitalna ghetto, to be isolated from the rest of the community. The ghetto was just a few streets barricaded with wooden fences, wire, and guards stationed with rifles. We lived in this little ghetto for a short time. The ghetto was very crowded. There were not enough bedrooms to sleep in and there was panic, always panic, not knowing what tomorrow would bring.

One day, the Nazis put out an order that who ever had an English passport would be allowed to go to England or Palestine. My sister Bronia and my brother-in-law David prepared going to Palestine.[9] My brother-in-law had a passport because he visited Palestine before the war. Because life in the ghetto was unbearable, they risked their lives, decided to make application although my parents were afraid that this was a German trick. This emigration did not materialize because the Germans, who made an exchange agreement with the English, went back on their promises and sent my sister and brother-in-law to Warsaw, Poland instead. There they were guarded day and night as hostages. From there, the Nazis sent them to Bergen-Belsen, in Germany, the concentration camp in which Anne Frank died; where people were dying daily.

I remember one day when my parents were baking bread. I was chosen, by the family, to go out from the ghetto to an office where the Germans distributed flour to bake bread. The family trusted me to go outside the ghetto to get some flour to bake the bread and to bring the ration cards to show how many people still are in the ghetto and to let them know how much flour to give out.

I had an armband with the Star of David. I put on my armband and took with me the numbers of people who were in the ghetto. I went to this office and two *gendarmes*, two guards stopped me. They took the rifles already pointed at me and said to me, "You are not allowed to go out from the ghetto. Where are you going?" So I showed the guards that I had permission and I am going to get flour to bake the bread. It didn't matter. "If we shoot a Jewish girl we will be rewarded," they said. At that time, the soldiers could shoot a Jewish girl, boy, man or woman and not even explain. Again they told me that they were permitted to do that. So they said to me, "You know what? If we have a chance to kill you we will."

The guards ordered me to stay against a wall and they pointed a rifle to shoot and kill me. Then, in the last minute, they changed their minds and asked me if I had some money with me. I said, "I had some money in my pockets." The soldiers said, "Give us the money." I gave them 20 Polish *Zlotys* and they agreed this one time they would spare my life. They took me back to the gate of the ghetto and they warned me,

"Beware! Don't go out anymore because now is a bad time." I went back to the ghetto shaken and frightened without flour to bake bread. It would not be my last near death experience.

CHAPTER FIVE

Deportation: Panic

The Nazis proclaimed there would be a deportation. Immediately, the Germans took the intelligentsia of our community. Doctors, lawyers, educators and Rabbis were marched into the forest to be murdered.[10] Panic ran through the ghetto again. Everything was secret. We didn't know whether we would go or something else worse might happen. So I said to my parents. "I will go with you because I am young and I will help you. I will be wherever you will be." The Nazis took us to an open assembly place; so many people in one place. We were surrounded by tall wooden electric poles and the lights. I remember it was hot. They made selections. That day, I resisted the black shirt Germans who were trying to separate me from my parents. I wanted to go with my parents but I was torn away from my family by a German Storm Trooper. This was August 17th, 1942.

I worked, with others, in a shoe factory called *Bata* from Czechoslovakia. The owners said we would be safe there but after the last deportation they had enough Polish people to work. So, they

Sister Shifra separated in the deportation.
Died in the Treblinka extermination camp.

sent us Jews back to the meeting place where the deportation was. There they would decide who should live and who should die. We couldn't take too many things out of the house. We took just a few belongings.

We walked through a check point where they examined work cards. The guard said that my card was not valid, anymore, but I still held on to my card. My sister Shifra had the same working card and a Nazi tore her card up. A German soldier came to me and he said to me, "You have a working card?" I said, "Yes! And I would like to be with my family."

A Jewish policeman stopped me and he said, "Look at her. This girl is young. Germany needs her for work." He looked at me from the top to the bottom. Those with working cards were ordered to stay on the right side. Those without should stay on the left side next to the train tracks. He took me by the hand and pulled me to the right side with those with working cards.

And that time, I saw my parents. I was happy to see my mother and father. But, I saw my parents, two brothers, Herschel and Shevech, and a sister Shifra for the last time. The Nazis moved them to a train, a cattle train, and they sent them to the extermination camp, Treblinka. This was not an internment camp. This was a death camp. There my loving parents, two brothers and one sister were gassed. There they all were cremated. I remained in the ghetto.

They closed the Szpitalna ghetto and moved many people to a second ghetto, the Glinice ghetto.[11] Rumors were that everybody who went to this ghetto was sent to Treblinka; the rumors were right. The Nazis came from Majdanek and proclaimed another ghetto for workers on the outskirts of the city; this was the Szkolna Ghetto. I managed to be moved there.[12]

CHAPTER SIX

The Radom Ghetto: Cutting Turf

After the deportation, I stayed in the ghetto. I had no choice. I was assigned to three jobs. My first was as a personal assistant for a German manufacturer both in his hardware factory and as a maid in his home for his family. The second job was in a depot where I, along with nine other women, were assigned the hard tiring task of separating feathers from the down comforters the Nazis stole from every Jewish home. The Nazis took me and another few girls and we collected pillows and comforters in a room of a school. In this room, we would have to sort the down from these linens that they sent to Germany for their families. The separated feathers were sent to Germany for the comfort of the German people to be warm while my Jewish friends and I had to suffer in the cold.

For my third job, in the ghetto, the guards took us out into the fields to cut turf. The Ukrainian guards, who worked together with the Nazis, took us to the ghetto and brought us back from the ghetto. The Germans needed us to go out and cut turf. Turf was a substitute for coal or wood used for heating the German houses. We worked very hard cutting turf. We cut the turf with our shovels in hard earth and we laid the turf out in the sun to dry in piles like the pyramids.

We had to cut a large amount of turf to satisfy the Nazis; otherwise we were punished by beatings over the head with a club. We had a *lager* or camp manager, who took care of us. It sticks in my mind that, one day, the crew didn't work hard enough at the cutting of the turf. The manager had a rubber stick. I was tired that day. I stood still standing for just a minute. The manager hit me over the head with a rubber stick and I fell down. Before they recounted Jewish workers, I had to get up and work again or else he would have murdered me.

In our ghetto rooms, we were very crowded living in one small room. We were lying at night like sardines on the floor and the hunger started because there was no food anymore. We were beaten, humiliated and starved but we worked and worked again. The ghetto was surrounded with a fence. My friends and I thought, if we could bring a sheet or a pillow case under our clothes to the ghetto fence perhaps a Polish woman on the other side will give us a piece of bread in trade. So we each took bed sheets and wrapped ourselves all

Brother Leon. Died in the Szpitalna ghetto.

around the body under our clothes, so that nobody, especially the guards should see if we carried something; if we took something. We found a Polish woman and managed to give a sheet and a pillow case in exchange for a piece of bread.

One day, one of my brothers, Leon, got very sick. Leon was sick and dying. He was in a small infirmary which was nothing more then a house where they took sick people to die. Leon was lying in a bed in a room unattended without a doctor or medicine. That day, I decided not to go to work. I risked my life by not going to work so I might stay with my brother and give him some water. I managed to stay with my brother to give him a little bit of water for his last hour. But the Ukrainian guards came in to this death chamber and said I had to be detained in a special shack with other people who also did not go to work. I was forced out of the room where my brother was. At the end, my brother Leon died from starvation and illness.

The Germans had a list of those who didn't go to work that day. With another few people, my guards kept me in this room with a window and bars. I said to my sister Regina, who came to the window from the outside, "I think this may be the last time I will see you because I have an intuition that tomorrow I won't be alive and they will kill us all." My sister Regina ran to the Jewish police. The policemen knew me, they knew my family, and they knew our bakery. She begged. Perhaps they could save one person, one life. The Jewish police decided they will risk their lives because they count the people and could get away with it.

In the middle of the night I heard the door to my prison open. The guards called my name. "Mania Frydman, Mania please come out." They took me to the office where they were stationed, put me on a bench to rest with a blanket and the police kept me the whole night.

In the morning, when it was time for the other prisoners to march toward their daily working places, the guards pushed me in between those working people hidden so I would go to work with them instead of being killed with the people who refused to go to work. I went in this group to work in a factory making pots and pans. The Nazis came to the ghetto in the morning and they killed everybody who didn't go to work. That is how I survived death once more.

I remember a friend who knew I was detained for not working and she heard everybody was shot. She ran up and down on the turf ground and cried, "Mania is dead, Mania is dead. They shoot her!" When I came back to cutting turf, I said to her, "Look, I am alive." Then she fainted, you know. She was so happy to see me.

CHAPTER SEVEN

The Szkolna Ghetto: Bela

Outstanding in my mind is the story of my sister Regina's little girl, my niece, named Bela. I, myself, a teenager at that time, was caught in this terrible hell on earth, not knowing if I would live from one day to the other. One day the Nazis forced us to move from the Szkolna ghetto to barracks located outside the city. When we came to the barrack there Bela was with my sister Regina and her husband, Motek. The Nazis forced my sister and her husband onto a truck to go to another camp near Pionki to an ammunition place for them to work leaving their daughter, Bela, behind. Bela was a smart and nice girl. She was five years old.

When the Nazis first came to Radom, we managed to hide Bela, and she survived two deportations to the death camp, Treblinka. On this day that Bela was taken away by the guards from her parents, they took the girl to a house nearby the barrack with another few children and a few elderly people to be killed; to be shot the next day in the morning.

Manya's
niece, Bela,
as infant
in carriage

Sister Regina
with Bela
Bela died
in Auschwitz
concentration
camp

I knew Bela was in the house. I was standing in the group to be sent out to work but I risked my life again. I was waiting outside the barrack to be assigned for work when I recognized a Ukrainian guard who previously had taken our group from the ghetto for the hard work of cutting turf. I approached him in desperation and I asked him, "Perhaps you want to save a Jewish child so later you will have a better conscience? This is my sister's child. She was raised in my home and I would like, perhaps, you should take her out of the house." The Ukrainian looked at me like I was demanding something impossible. And then, to my disbelief, he said he would try.

The guard told me to stay near the barrack. When the door opens he will give me Bela. I risked death because it was forbidden for me to wait near the house where the children were to be killed the next morning. Then, another Ukrainian guard came up to me and he did not know what was happening. He told me that this was not my place to stay there. My place was to stay with the group to go to be assigned to work. He pointed the rifle and he wanted to shoot me. So I said, "Wait, wait! Your friend told me to stay here." At that moment, the house door opened and the first guard came out with Bela. He dismissed the angry guard and he said, "Hide the girl wherever you can."

Quickly, I grabbed the child. And there, close by, on the assembly place near the barrack, there were woven baskets, long tall woven baskets. I hid Bela outside under a tall woven basket which we made for grenades for the German Army. I said to Bela, "I put you under the woven basket and don't move because the basket will shake. If the basket shakes, the Germans will know you are here and, if they grab you, they will put you with the people they take to the train to shoot and be dead." Bela said, "I will obey. I will not move the basket." She understood and obeyed. From now on, Bela became my responsibility. I became responsible for the little girl's life; my sister Regina's daughter; my Bela.

When Bela was safe for a short while, I ran to a Jewish policeman and I told him this story. "I cannot be in this group to go out to work because I just saved a little girl and I would like to take care of her. I would like to have a job in the barrack like, for instance, cleaning or cooking to be able to take care of Bela." So he agreed. He assigned me to work in the barrack. But it was dangerous. When the Nazis went away they came back very often to count how many people were in each barrack. I had to teach Bela how she should hide in the barrack when the Nazis came to count us. When I saw the Germans coming, I would give Bela a wink of my eye. Bela knew already to hide under the bunk; the lowest bunk. And she covered her little hand over her mouth so she shouldn't give out a sound because instantly they would find her. We would be, everybody in the barrack would be, killed.

By the way, I was lucky to be assigned for work to clean the barracks so I could take care of Bela. Bela did not receive the small portion of bread which they gave us. Bela was not supposed to exist. So I was with another sister, Pola, at this time. Pola worked in a special house sewing together German army uniforms but we lived close together. I saw her sometimes. My sister Pola and I shared our pieces of precious bread with Bela. And the people in the barrack were not too happy because Bela caused a problem and danger but nobody said not one word. Though we in the barrack knew of the danger Bela caused us, we looked at her like she would be the greatest treasure on earth; the only child left to tell our story. Bela gave us hope and courage to go on with our lives in those horrible conditions.

One day, I learned that there would be a deportation to Majdanek concentration camp in Poland near Lublin by cattle car. My sister Pola and I would be in this transport. And Bela, I could not take her. We heard the rumors that in Majdanek camp the Nazis killed, in one day, 20,000 Jewish people and the crematoriums were burning day and night.

I later met a woman, Sally, who was in the cattle train going to Majdanek.[13] She once lived in Warsaw and was transferred to Radom from Majdanek to work in a printing factory. When Sally noticed that the cattle trains were leaving Radom in the direction of Majdanek, she told me she was not going back again to that killing camp. Sally took out a razor blade and wanted to cut her wrists. I was standing nearby with other girls and I took the blade from her hand and said, "Sally, you don't do this. You have to wait to see what's going to be with our lives, and maybe we will all live," and she agreed not to take her life.

In Majdanek, I knew everybody is dying. How can I take the child with me? I was afraid to take Bela with me because they would shoot her right away. The Nazis didn't know that there was a child in the barrack. They would ask, "Where is a child coming from?"

Brother Itsik who took Bela from Manya.
Died the day of liberation in
Mathausen concentration camp.

I had a teenage brother, Itsik, working in an ammunition factory near the barrack. There were wires dividing my barrack place and the ammunition factory where my brother worked. I knew my Itsik could not take Bela into an all men's barrack but he had a woman friend who would take her into the women's barrack with the rest of the girls. So, I notified him he should come by the wires. I saw Itsik through the wires and told him that I will be deported. And I told him I could not take Bela with. Maybe she should remain in Radom. Perhaps tomorrow the Russians will come. Perhaps, after tomorrow, he will be liberated.

There was not much time to think because the guards were all around. I explained the situation to the child. I gave Bela my last hug and kiss. She looked at me with tears in her eyes and said that she will obey again. I lifted the wires, pushed her through the other side. I shipped her to my brother Itsik, and from then on she became his responsibility.

But the saga was near an end for Bela. I learned later, as the Russian army approached, Bela and the rest of the workers of the ammunition factory were forced to walk many kilometers to Auschwitz concentration camp. On the way, a guard told Bela to go on a horse drawn wagon with people who could no longer walk. Bela said, "No! I don't want to go on the horse and wagon. I want to walk with all the people because I want to live." The people who could not walk any longer, the Nazis took them aside and killed them.

For Bela the saga ended. Bela walked to Auschwitz and at the gate of Auschwitz she was taken away to the gas chamber and the crematorium. The little girl was taken away to the "place of no return." Bela did not survive. At the gate of Auschwitz, they took her away to be murdered along with one and half million Jewish children. And I went on to Majdanek. This was 1943.

CHAPTER EIGHT

Majdanek: So Many Shoes

The Nazis moved my sister Pola and me to Majdanek concentration camp.[14] When I came to Majdanek, I went into a room. I still had a few belongings. I had little belongings; belongings from my house which I took with me. These last belongings were taken from me. They took away everything from me. They took away my shoes. They gave us all too small shoes, which for me was very painful. Without socks it became difficult for me to walk. I went into a room to undress with my sister Pola. We were there to help each other undress. We stood naked.

I had a small gold ring and little gold earrings in my ears which my mother gave me. The SS woman guard told me that if I did not give them up she would cut them from my ears. Then, Pola and I were separated. I went to another room and I dressed myself with a striped uniform, a prison uniform to wear with a prison number. From now

Sister Pola survived Majdanek, Plaszow,
and Ravensbruck concentration camps.
She immigrated to Israel.

on there would be no name for me anymore just a number. No name for me anymore.

The guards chased us out for roll call in any kind of weather to make sure no one escaped. In the cold weather, I was standing in mud up to my ankles and my feet got very, very cold. It was impossible to escape because the camp was surrounded with electric wire. If I would touch the wire, I would be electrocuted. And then we started to work again at those woven baskets for grenades. We became like *arbeit heflingers*, work prisoners.

In this camp, we met the fifty young girls who were witnesses to murder. The Germans ordered fifty Jewish girls to sort the clothing and the shoes from the dead bodies; so many shoes. The girls were eyewitnesses to the killing of many Jewish people and the girls were left to work in the magazines sorting clothing and shoes after the gassings and cremations. We were new and not witnesses to people killed. So one night the girls came to us and they said if the Germans come and ask if you know about the killings don't say that you heard. Say that you don't know.

Then it came to the liquidation of Majdanek.[15] The Russians approached and the Nazis emptied the camp. When the camp was liquidated the fifty girls were sent to Auschwitz to be killed; the eyewitnesses to the slaughter of thousands. Pola and I and the other girls were transported to the Plaszow concentration camp nearer to Krakow, Poland. This was a camp of many selections and brutal killings.

CHAPTER NINE

Plaszow: Brutality

They liquidated Majdanek with cattle trains. There were so many people crushed in the wagon. We couldn't breathe. With no food and with just nothing we came into Krakow, to Plaszow and this was a terrible camp of many killings.[16] This was the camp where Oskar Schindler managed to save more then a thousand Jewish people.

It was in Plaszow that I wanted to tell you about the selections. One day Dr. Joseph Mengele came to this camp from Auschwitz. They called him the "evil angel" of this camp. And he said to us that everybody should undress naked and pass by in the front of him. We had to undress and parade in front of Mengele and he made selections. Who will be still able to work will live and who is weak will die. And when he noticed on a body a pimple or something, something wrong, right away that person was selected by Mengele to move to the side to be killed.

And, in this same camp, there was a commandant, Goeth. He was aiming and shooting at men, women, and children who passed close by.

I saw Commandant Goeth on a big white horse shooting people right and left for sport. I had to escape and hide. I started to run and managed to hide.

We were working in a hardware factory near Schindler on the outskirts of Plaszow with a boss and overseer. One day the Nazis took us back to the Plaszow camp to show us they caught a Jewish commandant and his wife trying to escape. They hanged them in the center of the place and we walked around them in a circle to look at them hanging dead. The Nazis said we should know there is no escape because they are going to catch us and do with us the same thing.

And in Plaszow too, they had roll call and we went out a few times every day from the barracks to be counted, only to be sure if somebody didn't escape. One time a girl couldn't come quickly. She remained in the barrack because she didn't feel good. She was shaking and very sick. So the Nazis counted the girl missing. That day it was raining creating so much mud. The ground was soft because some parts of Plaszow used to be a cemetery. The guards told us to kneel down in the mud for hours and not even to shake our heads. All of us were punished because the missing girl did not come in time for the count.

CHAPTER TEN

Auschwitz-Birkenau: Fear

Once again the Russian front approached. The Nazis didn't want us to be liberated to the Russians. Wherever the Nazis went, from one camp to the other, they took us with them. After Plaszow, they took us to Auschwitz, to the Birkenau death camp and we were there in the Gypsy camp where the Gypsies lived in *Lager* C but the Gypsies were no more.[17]

In Birkenau, also, the Nazis called roll call and we stood very still. I was standing doing nothing but staring at the chimneys of the crematoria. I wondered why they didn't give me a tattoo number. Was it because they didn't know what they wanted to do with us? I thought if they didn't give a number that I would have to go to the gas chambers; so why no number? My humiliation became complete, in Birkenau, by shaving off all my hair from my head. The guard took us to the showers. I was shivering and thinking that this was the end of life but instead of gas came out water. I became infected with a blood infection and a high fever. I was in need of an aspirin or some medicine.

I knew there was an infirmary in a small house near the barrack and I decided to go there to ask for an aspirin with the hope that I would feel better. So I went to the room where they gave out medicine. The camp doctor was deciding to treat me or not. Through a small window, he saw Dr. Mengele approaching. Mengele made it a point to visit the camp infirmary occasionally to select sick people to kill in his experiments. The camp doctor warned me of Mengele's approach and he showed me a side door for escape. He said to me, "Go out. I cannot give you nothing because Mengele is coming in. If he will see you, he will kill you." And I ran out without the medicine.

So, Dr. Mengele passed through and I escaped because I knew he was taking some girls for experiments. I ran to the barrack quickly. I was very thin and slipped easily under the lowest bunk. Mengele came and he didn't see me. I hid successfully and once again I survived death.

Then in came the *hauptman,* the same boss from Plaszow from the hardware factory, to take eighty girls, including me, out of Birkenau to another camp. Like Schindler took his people to Czechoslovakia, he took us out to Germany, near Flossenburg, to work for him. He moved his building business to Germany because of the Russian advancing army.

CHAPTER ELEVEN

Gundersdorf: Near Death

As the Russians approached the German army, I was moved to a camp called Gundersdorf in Germany. From Birkenau to Gundersdorf, this was like a death camp. We had to work near the train tracks loading and unloading trains and doing the most difficult tasks. In this camp I worked very hard loading on trains heavy electric cables and poles. I carried electric poles with another girl, one end on my shoulder and one end on her shoulder in bitter cold weather. It was winter time then and I was very cold. My hands got frostbite from touching the hardware. And I said to the girls, "Oh, G-d help us. Why do the Germans want to kill us? What do they want from us?" And the cruel answer was, "Because we were Jewish. We did nothing. We are innocent and they want to kill us."

Every night we came to the barrack from hard work and they gave us a little bit of soup with a small portion of bread just to have one bite. At that time, the hunger caught up with us. We were very, very hungry. I stood in line with my plate to get some soup. I wanted to be the first to get a little bit of soup and, hopefully, get a piece of potato or something. I approached the soup kettle. I thought maybe underneath there will be a little potato. The soup was like water and not a piece of potato.

The next day I was in line to be the last so perhaps there would be in the soup a piece of potato or a carrot at the bottom of the pot. But when I approached the soup pot, there was nothing left for me, not even soup. And I went to the bunk without the blanket, without straw just to lie down on the wooden barrack floor. I went to sleep on the wooden floor of the barrack hungry only to start another day of hard work.

In Gundersdorf, in this camp, there was an incident. My job was to carry raw potatoes to the German kitchen for their meals. I was wearing my striped uniform. I managed to take two potatoes from the German kitchen hidden in my striped dress. I took the two raw potatoes to the camp barrack. I was so hungry. I took potatoes to share with the girls in the barrack pieces from the two potatoes. Coming back to the barrack, I was searched and the guards found the potatoes. The guard gave me over to the camp commandant. And that *lagerfuher* took me to his barrack and I was punished. He beat me with a black rubber club over my body. The Nazi commandant beat me twenty-five times with the rubber stick and when I came back to the barrack, the girls helped me by putting some water on my wounds. They helped me survive and go on further. I didn't believe I would live much longer but I promised myself that, if I survived the war, I would never be cold and hungry again.

By that time, we lost any hope but we promised each other to go on and let's see what will happen to us because, already, it was so bad. I was afraid nobody will be left and nobody will be able to tell this story. Let somebody survive and let's, with all our strength, go further. After being in Gundersdorf for six months, the Nazis had to liquidate the camp.

CHAPTER TWELVE

Ravensbruck: A Crumb of Hope

In Gundersdorf, a train was waiting; another wooden cattle train. We were packed in and taken to Ravensbruck concentration camp in Germany.[18] It was a journey to Ravensbruck of six days and six nights without bread and water. It seemed like forever. In the train, there were many people, so crowded. This was a long journey of death. The hunger was already too much. We were skeletons, already, from starvation. There were lice. They ate us up alive. We had to shake out the lice from our uniforms and we were weak.

There was a small barred window in the train and I worked my way over to the window where I saw a group of German soldiers along the road. I don't know if they went to the front or they came back from the front. I shouted out to them, "Could you give me a piece of bread that I could share with the girls in the car?" A German soldier, to my wonder, took out some bread and he gave me, through the bars, a piece of bread which I shared with the other girls. We sat down crowded on the filthy wagon floor and every one of the girls came over. Everybody had a crumb of bread and this was a help to all of us.

In this Ravensbruck camp, I asked myself again, "Why do they want to kill me?" Is the only reason that I was born Jewish? I wanted to die so many times. I lost my hope but as the war was nearing to an end, I was determined to live. I was afraid that the war would end soon and no one would be left to tell what happened to us.

CHAPTER THIRTEEN

Rechlin and Retzow: Hunger

We were not too long at Ravensbruck, maybe a week, because the war was close to an end. Again, the Nazis didn't want to leave us. Again, with the Russian army advancing, the Nazis sought to delay their defeat and our liberation. They heard that the Americans were near and believed American troops would treat them better.

Fearful of the Russian army for the thousands of Russian soldier prisoners murdered by their hands, the Nazis fled toward the American front. They did not want us to go to the Russians. The Nazis ordered us on a "death march" because they told us they wanted to take us to an American front.[19] Hitler gave an order that a "death march" should be part of his "final solution." They took us with them for more killing and suffering. On the march, the Nazis were relentless in their efforts to kill all remaining Jews.

We stopped at two other small camps, Rechlin and Retzow.[20] In Rechlin, the Germans threw out from their kitchen stale bread and I was outside to see this. I said to myself that before the march started again, maybe, I'll grab some bread and have bread for the journey. I fell on the ground to grab some bread and on top of me, it seemed, fell hundreds of more inmates to get a piece of bread and I was underneath. I could not breathe. And I said to myself, now it will be the end because I will suffocate. But one German guard shot in the air and the people dispersed. I came out from this suffocation alive. I lost the bread and I did not have any bread. Afterwards, I heard bombing and shooting and then I was chased out into the death march walking and falling from weakness. But, once again, death was not for me.

**Brother Shevech.   Died in the Treblinka
extermination camp.**

CHAPTER FOURTEEN

The Death March: Resistance

On the death march, we were marching and marching and marching. I thought that every step would be my last. Once we stopped, and then our guards said they will give us packages from the Red Cross which the Red Cross donated. And, to my surprise, they gave me a package. There was some beans and something else but I looked at the food and I couldn't eat. I was delirious. I couldn't swallow. Everything felt like death was inside me. I just left the package aside because, if I would eat something, I was afraid to die. My intestines were already dead. So, I didn't eat anything. And, I started to march again. Bodies were piling up as we walked. Whoever fell to the ground during the march would be shot. The Nazis would shoot them. I thought that this was the end again.

At night it was dark. We passed a forest. My friend, Hana, and I walked near the forest and I said that I could not walk any further because it would kill me. I looked around so that no guard would see us slip into the forest and we walked away from hundreds of women. The guards didn't see us sneak into the forest while the death march continued.

We managed to go into the forest further and further and we sat under a tree to wait for I don't know what; the Germans; the Americans; the Russians; death. And we waited four days and three nights under the tree. The air was cold and heavy. The nights were very dark pierced by the sounds of bombardments and shootings. I thought I would not live to see the daylight again. I heard shooting and many bombs falling around us and I said again this will be my end because nobody is here in the forest. If I won't die from the bomb, I will die from starvation.

But on the fourth day, the Russians came into the forest looking for prisoners of war, German prisoners of war and they found Hana and I sitting under a tree in the forest. On May 1st, 1945, I was liberated from this hell on earth by the Russian Army. I weighed very little and I was very weak.

The Russian soldiers took me into a house and tried to give me some milk, some food but I still couldn't eat anything. I was resting there in this farm house for a while and in came another few girls, also, from nearby and we rested together. We took off our filthy torn uniforms, our striped pajamas, and put on dresses which we found in the farm house and little by little we began to eat something. I don't know from malnutrition and how my body was affected but many of us girls had problems every month. Later I heard that the Nazis put something into the food, some medicine to the soup so the girls should not have the menstruations and at that time it stopped.

Coming to my senses, I then realized and felt the impact of the tragedy. Once I had a home, parents, family and now I am left alone, all alone. The allies said to us "You are free. We came to liberate you." I said in Polish, "Thank you, but I am sorry, the liberation came much too late for the millions of fathers, mothers, brothers, sisters, and children who went to the gas chambers." The soldiers who liberated us saw the gas chambers and the ashes. Those ashes of our loved ones still cry out to us survivors and beg us to bear witness to the world of what happened.

The girls and I talked about returning to Poland. We said when we have more strength we will go to Poland. I thought, perhaps, I could return to Radom and find somebody from my family.

CHAPTER FIFTEEN

Return to Radom: Delay

On the way to Radom, to Poland, I got sick with Typhus Fever and my temperature was very high. The girls helped me go into a hospital near Stettin, Germany. It isn't far from Berlin. But the hospital didn't have food or medicine so the staff advised one girl to go to the Russian commandant to tell them that there is a Jewish girl that has survived the concentration camps and they should bring some medicine, something for the infection, for the high fever. Right away, a delegation came from the Russian army. They brought medicine and some food and they told me that when I go out from the hospital they will come for me and take me to recuperate in their barrack.

When I was in the hospital, I had a high fever. I had a vision and in this vision I saw my mother come into my room. I said, "Mother, you were supposed to be cremated. We were cut off from the whole world so we only knew of rumors. I learned through rumors that you were dead. Somebody came from Treblinka and this is how I learned." And my mother said, "No! I am alive and somebody told me you were in this hospital and I wanted to come and tell you that you have to survive again because who will tell your story. You have to tell the world this story; your story and the story of the Jewish people and what they went through; the tortures, the murders, what happened." When I woke up, I asked the nurse, "Where is my mother?" So she said, "No! There was no mother and this was only a hallucination."

CHAPTER SIXTEEN

Destination Radom: Radom No More

I survived this Typhus and I went to Radom. After I recuperated, I went to Radom by foot, by horse drawn wagon, because all the tracks were bombed from the war. Finally, I was able to take a train from Poznan to Radom but the city was not a safe place to stay. There was still anti-Semitism and the Poles it was rumored killed every day another survivor and I had to go to the funerals.[21] Soon, I learned my sisters Regina and Pola were in a displaced persons camp in Germany. It was not too long a time before I left Radom, Poland for Stuttgart, Germany.

CHAPTER SEVENTEEN

Displacement: When is Free, Free?

After only two weeks in Radom, I started a journey back to Germany. A truck took me to Berlin, and with a train I went to Stuttgart, Germany into a displaced persons camp that the United Nations Relief and Rehabilitation Administration (UNRRA) had established for the Holocaust survivors.[22] My sisters and some friends and I were there. We rested and recuperated in apartments assigned to us. In this displaced persons camp for the first time in six years we had a nice bed to sleep in, enough food, and I didn't see rifles pointed at me any more all the time. I was free to walk the streets. We observed the Jewish holidays and we had a Rabbi and a Cantor. In this place, most importantly, we didn't see the Nazi Swastika hanging over our heads making us fearful any minute to be dead. I just waited and recuperated. I was in a displaced persons camp from 1945, when the war ended, to 1948 until I fully recovered. In that place, I gained enough strength to be sent to a hospital to

Manya in Stuttgart West
Displaced Persons camp.

have operations on a ruptured stomach, the result of the damage of hard work, starvation and thirst. I was determined that, after I recuperated fully, I wanted to be an independent person. I wanted to fit into society. This was my determination not to let myself be pitied by anyone. I wanted to be a human being again.

DP · DP · DP · DP · DP

DISPLACED PERSONS PASS
and ex-Political Prisoner from
Concentration Camps

FRYDMAN   Mania .... may be absent
        Name

from .... Stuttgart West   668
            camp Name   No.

from .... hrs to .... hrs
and may circulate within an area not over .... km from such camp

No. 582

Signature
UNRRA Director

DP · DP · DP · DP · DP

Manya's Displaced Persons Camp Pass

72

CHAPTER EIGHTEEN

The West: Return to Normalcy

I had an aunt who immigrated to Montreal, Canada. In 1948, she sent me and my sister Regina, an affidavit to join her and live with her family. I went to Canada and arrived by boat in Halifax, Nova Scotia. A delegation from UNRRA came for us and then we took a train to Montreal. We met up with surviving relatives and I was happy to be with them. But, after a while, I wanted a life of my own, to be independent. At last I was free to marry and have children, to fulfill the dream I had as a teenage girl playing outside my home and my family's bakery in Radom before the war. I met my future husband, Rafael. He was also a survivor. We got married.

My sister Regina remarried. Her new husband had relatives in Philadelphia and so they went to Philadelphia to live. At that time, I had two sisters living in Israel, Pola and Bronia. So, my sister Regina in Philadelphia said, "Oh, two sisters in Israel and one in Montreal. You are in Canada.

Sister Regina survived Auschwitz,
Bergen-Belsen concentration camps.
She settled in Montreal, Canada.

won't you please come so we can be together?" So, I made a decision to be with my sister Regina in Philadelphia.

In 1958, Rafael and I moved to Philadelphia with our two small children, Marvin and Sylvia. In the beginning, we lived with my sister and her husband. While Rafael looked for steady work it was very difficult to find an apartment of our own. Soon we found a nice couple who rented us an apartment near Roosevelt Boulevard in N.E. Philadelphia. Later, we looked for and found a home of our own in the same location near my sister.

Rafael started to work to make a good living. He was a house painter, a decorator. We sent our two children to Hebrew School to get the Jewish education we both missed. Rafael and I were determined to work hard to support the children through elementary, middle school and high school because we didn't have the privilege of an education. We managed to send them to college and they both graduated. They are intelligent and educated and I am very proud of them. They are good children.

Rafael and I joined a conservative synagogue near our home, Oxford Circle Jewish Community Center (OCJCC). We celebrated the holidays and being Jewish. We did this to hold onto the traditions for the children. With respect to the memory of our parents who died in Treblinka, I joined an organization, the Association of Jewish Holocaust Survivors, which is an association consisting of members from all over Eastern Europe. Everyone who is here belongs to this organization from all the countries of Eastern Europe. We are very active. We raise money for the Jewish National fund and for bond drives. I am the secretary of the lady's group.

Manya and Rafael Perel

CHAPTER NINETEEN

Witness To History: Speaking Out

I started to talk about the Holocaust but not in the beginning. It was too difficult. I thought the people here, the American born, (and I don't blame them) they wouldn't understand the tragedy of my life. They wouldn't comprehend those tortures and what we went through. So I did not talk. The survivors, we talked between each other, but we did not talk especially to other people. Then, when I approached aging, I started to speak out on the Holocaust because this is history. This has to be documented.

Some people deny that there was a Holocaust; that the Holocaust ever happened. We are the eyewitnesses and we are alive and we know the Holocaust happened to six million Jewish people, one and a half million who were Jewish children, along with millions of non-Jews. I started to be active, to talk to schools and to give my testimony so that all people should remember. I survived because I was afraid that nobody would survive, that nobody will be left to tell this story. I can assure you, if the war would take another two or three weeks, I wouldn't be here to tell this story because if I wouldn't die of a bullet, I would die of starvation. This catastrophe, the Holocaust was almost the end for me. This was meant to be that I should survive and tell this story.

Today, I have nightmares. I have many, many nightmares. I never want to go back to Radom, not any more, because there is no one there for me. Just to go back and see the concentration camps that I saw in the Holocaust Museum in Washington D.C., when I was there, would be very painful.

Sister Bronia survived
Bergen-Belsen concentration camp.
She immigrated to Israel.

CHAPTER TWENTY

Today: The Final Resistance

During the years, time and time again, when I have conversations with people who did not live through World War II, many will ask why the Jews did not resist the Nazis. I try to explain that we resisted in every way we could while the murderous Nazi death machine was pointed at each and every one of us. Our weapons were our bare hands, our minds, our courage and our faith. I, personally, resisted by forming a solidarity with my parents and siblings until I was forcibly taken away to work in slave labor. I resisted by helping my brother in the ghetto hold on to life until his last breath. I resisted by caring for my sister's daughter Bela, holding on to hope that she would survive to tell her story. I resisted by stealing bread and potatoes to share with my friends. I resisted by risking my life, time and time again.

The Jewish people actively resisted during the Holocaust. The Jewish people resisted by creating sabotage, rebellion, and uprisings when and wherever possible. They fought to the last drop of blood against the Nazi machinery. And, finally, we survivors resisted with our minds. The Nazis could not crush our spirit, our faith, or our love for life and humanity. **<u>Everyone who survived</u>** successfully resisted the Nazis and their "Final Solution." The "Final Solution" it turns out was the Nazi German ideology that turned on itself and became the destiny of the Third Reich, never to be heard from again.

Some people question how long we will talk about the Holocaust. Some people even deny that the Holocaust even happened. My answer is, "How can I forget?" After so many years, I still have so many nightmares of the Nazis wanting to run after me and they want to kill me. How can we forget the suffering and that so many innocent people lost their lives? Never again should evil and monstrous murderers like Hitler and the Nazis be permitted to rule a country.

And how many books are written on the Holocaust? How many movies are produced or how many museums are built? All these material things cannot depict the real tragedy of my suffering and the suffering of the Jewish people.

Someday, I will rest better knowing that my children and the tens of thousands of students I have spoken to have promised to take over my task and carry on my legacy from generation to generation. Let's always remember the Holocaust.

Please remember that history may repeat itself if we allow ourselves to forget.

EPILOGUE

I have a message: first of all to the people in the world that they should not be prejudiced. The Nazis came for the Jewish people and five million others. Next time, if you will be silent, something evil may come for you. We have to speak out because we only have one life to enjoy freedom. My determination, at the present time, is to continue to teach the lessons of the Holocaust in schools and colleges so the lessons should be there for those who come after us not to forget. Remember, such a horrible human catastrophe should never ever happen again.

I believe that we must help to support Israel. Had there been an internationally recognized Jewish state, in 1939, I believe the Holocaust would never have happened. I am an active speaker in the Holocaust Awareness Museum and Education Center's survivor outreach program, giving my testimony to hundreds of schools and organizations and thousands of students through out the years.

I hope that my life will be an example for others not to take life for granted, not to be prejudiced towards others, and to respect one another. My prayers go out to all mankind for a

Mark, Jeffrey, Rina and Sylvia Wagman

Andrew, Marvin, Lois, Daniel and Evan Perel

world at peace, a world that will not forget so that such a tragedy will never repeat itself. I have dedicated my life to bearing witness to young and old.

Since the war, I managed to get married to my husband, Rafael, and have good children, Marvin and Sylvia, a daughter-in-law, Lois, a son-in-law Mark and six grandchildren, Evan, Yael, Andrew, Daniel, Rina, and Jeffrey, all of whom I am very proud. They all received the education which I was denied and they have promised to take over my task and carry on my legacy from generation to generation.

Manya Frydman Perel

Manya Frydman Perel, a recipient of countless awards and letters of commendation from United States Presidents, dignitaries, State Governors, and community leaders finds her greatest joy and satisfaction in the letters and e-mail from students to whom she has presented her testimony. The following pages represent a sampling of their appreciation over the decades.

MJA

IN APPRECIATION

May 1975

Dear Mrs. Perel,

    I am in awe of you and I thank you for sharing your story with us. I cannot imagine how you are able to be so loving and forgiving. Your story touched my heart and throughout your visit the tears just flowed from my eyes.

    I admire you for your strength and wisdom. I will always remember you and, as I live my life, I vow that I will not stand silent when I am faced with hatred and evil.

    God bless you with the courage and strength to continue speaking out for all the victims of the Holocaust.

Most sincerely,

F.E. S.

IN APPRECIATION

Dear Mrs. Perel,

I was one of your escorts at the Holocaust symposium at my High School. I just wanted to write to you and thank you so much for sharing your story with us. It meant so much to me and many other students came up to me and asked about you as everyone was impressed by your speech in the auditorium. Your survivor spirit inspired me to want to help with peace around the world. I hope no one ever has to go through the horrors you experienced and, if they do, I hope they can come away with your amazing survivor spirit. Your story inspired so many and made the Holocaust a more "real" event to all those who heard you speak. I am so grateful that we had the extra time to talk before your presentation. I love how energetic and full of life you are. I hope I always have the same passion for living that you do. Thank you so much for everything.

Love,

L. F.

IN APPRECIATION

September 1991

Dear Mrs. Perel,

Your visit to our classroom yesterday was inspiring and life changing for many of the students.

I appreciate how difficult it is to relive those horrific times, but I praise your courage for doing it.

You are very special to us and we will always remember you, your story, and the horror of the Holocaust so that it may never happen again.

M.P. and the 8th Grade class

IN APPRECIATION

October 2005

Dear Mrs. Perel,

Thank you so very much for coming to my school and sharing your story with me. Your story was amazing. I am sorry that you had to go through that great tragedy where so many lives were tortured and lost. We must never let such a thing happen ever again. You are a brave woman and I am grateful that you have shared your story with me. I look up to people like you. You are a hero. I will always remember your legacy.

Sincerely,

K.R.

IN APPRECIATION

January 2011

Dear Mrs. Perel,

    I want to start with thanking you for coming to my class and sharing your story. Your story opened my eyes to the true horror of the Holocaust. I have watched movies like "The Boy in the Striped Pajamas" and read books like "Night" but actually meeting a survivor and hearing the terrible details from a real person made me understand the true reality of the Holocaust. I realized that everything that happened was just evil and inhumane. Thank you for having the courage and motivation to share your story. I will never forget it.

Sincerely,

C. C.

NOTES

1. Lipton, Alfred, ed. The Book of Radom (New York: Liberty Press, 1963), "Poland had the greatest accumulation of houses of worship and Jewish learning…and Radom indeed was the jewel in the crown of Polish Jewry." p.vii.
2. ibid., "There were forty Jewish bakeries in Radom. The largest were Friedman's (Frydman's)…etc." p.18.
3. ibid., "Under the influence of Nazi ideology anti-Semitic bands turned to violence which came to a head in 1936." p.33.
4. Katz, Shmuel, Lone Wolf: A Biography of Vladimir Jabotinsky (New York: Baricade Books, 1996), A liberal Zionist revisionist repeatedly warned Polish Jews, as late as 1938, that they must leave Poland for Palestine., p.6.
5. Dwork, Deborah, ed., Voices & Views: A History of the Holocaust (New York: The Jewish Foundation for the Righteous, 2002), "Germany expelled 17, 000 German Jews (Polish origins) sending them to the Polish border." p.145.
6. The Book of Radom, "All Jews over ten years were ordered to wear a white arm band with a blue Jewish 'Star of David.'" p.40.
7. ibid., "Under a rationing system, Jews were allowed only one half as much food as Poles. In reality they received less." p.41.
8. ibid., "In March 1941…(the) governor of Radom issued a decree establishing two separate ghettos in Radom…" p.42.
9. ibid., "Hopes in connection with a move to Palestine never materialized as Germans reneged…" p.59.
10. ibid., That day the Germans deported the members of the Jewish council…destined for Treblinka." p. 57.
11. ibid., "90% of the Glinice ghetto was liquidated. The rest were sent for forced labor…" pg.60.
12. ibid., p.58.
13. ibid., "In May of 1943, 100 men and women were brought to the ghetto from the concentration camp Majdanek." p. 62.
14. .ibid., "In March 1944, the SS…relocated several hundred men and women…driven to the railroad station. It was later learned that their destination was the extermination camp in Majdanek." p.64.
15. Voices & Views, "In July 1944, Majdanek was the first large camp to be vacated." Pg.129.
16. The Book of Radom, "In April 1944, …men and women from Majdanek from Radom were transferred to the Plaszow camp." p..69.
17. ibid., "In August 1944, the Plaszow camp was evacuated. Ten thousand women were sent to Auschwitz." p. 69.
18. ibid., "…Radom women were transferred from Auschwitz to Ravensbruck." p..69.
19. Voices and Views, "…January 1945, the remaining…(Ravensbruck women) were herded onto roads leading west. Thousands perished during those forced marches." p.129.
20. http://www.kulturportal-mv.de. "Women from the Ravensbruck concentration camp were brought here by force."
21. Voices & Views, "In Poland, the country that had become the graveyard of Europe's Jews…anti-Jewish violence was all too common. As many as 2,000 Jews were killed between 1944-1947. Most were killed when they returned to their home towns looking for family." p.589.
22. The Book of Radom, In August, 1945…Jews were transferred…to their new location in Stuttgart." p.85.